P9-CFG-443

Under, Over, By the Clover

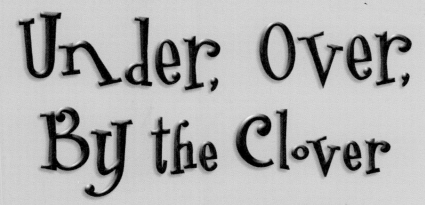

What Is a Preposition?

To Patrick, Clare, Fiona, and Luke,
who are **BEYOND** good.   —B.P.C.

To the indomitable Spot
                          —B.G.

Preposition: **A** word that connects a noun or pronoun to other words in a sentence.

Under, Over, By the Clover

What Is a Preposition?

by Brian P. Cleary

illustrated by Brian Gable

CAROLRHODA BOOKS, INC. / MINNEAPOLIS

beside the chair—

under,
over,
by the
clover,

About,
above,
or next to
Rover.

They tell us

time and also place,

During recess

after school,

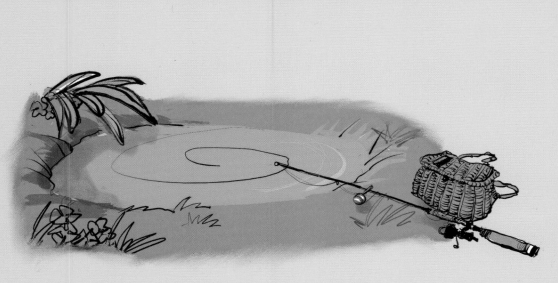

in
between
the pond
and pool.

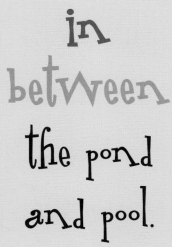

That prepositions aren't correct to end a sentence **with**.

But write your sentence carefully,
and you'll discover that

Ending
with a
preposition

is often where it's at.

Prepositions give direction

Like, doctors rushed to Rhonda's wrecked shin.

Or charlie danced
the charleston
over on the green,

Down, beyond,
around the bend,
along the old
ravine.

Through
the yard
of Chris, the hippie.

Go Pitt!!

Like, Paul's **from** Pittsburgh,

Way up there,

I hid beneath
the old oak chair—

Into, inside, from the zoo,

Home by way
of Timbuktu.

when
where
how

They tell the
whens, the wheres,
the hows,

'cause that's
their special
mission,

and help to link
the other words—

that's what's a preposition!

So, what is a
Preposition?
Do you know?

ABOUT THE AUTHOR & ILLUSTRATOR

BRIAN P. CLEARY is the author of several other picture books, including <u>A Mink, a Fink, a Skating Rink: What Is a Noun?</u>, <u>To Root, to Toot, to Parachute: What Is a Verb?</u> and <u>Hairy, Scary, Ordinary: What Is an Adjective?</u> He lives in Cleveland, Ohio.

BRIAN GABLE lives and works in Toronto, Ontario, with his wife, Teresa, and two children, Kristin and Stephen.

Text copyright © 2002 by Brian P. Cleary
Illustrations copyright © 2002 by Brian Gable

Carolrhoda Books, Inc., a division of Lerner Publishing Group
241 First Avenue North, Minneapolis, MN 55401 U.S.A.

Website address: www.lernerbooks.com

Library of Congress Cataloging-in-Publication Data

Cleary, Brian P., 1959—
     Under, over, by the clover : what is a preposition? / by Brian P.
Cleary ; illustrated by Brian Gable.
       p.   cm. — (Words are categorical)
     ISBN 1—57505—524—4 (lib. bdg. : alk. paper)
1. English language—Prepositions—Juvenile literature. [1. English
language—Prepositions.] I. Gable, Brian, 1949— ill. II. Title.
PE1335.C581 2002
428.2—dc21   2001001263

Manufactured in the United States of America
1 2 3 4 5 6 - JR - 07 06 05 04 03 02